D1171111

Art into landscape
Landscape into art

EUROPEAN BEECH TREES

A powerful composition approaching grandeur and the sublime in plant life. For centuries double rows of European Beech have been planted along certain roads of Northern Europe. These, found near Arnhem, Holland, show eloquently how trees growing only ten to twelve meters apart can develop to great size.

This scene generates its visual power through repetition of massive trunks soaring vertically for an extended distance and through continuity of receding space.

Art into landscape
Landscape into art
A.E. BYE • Landscape Architect

PDA Publishers Corporation
Mesa, Arizona

ACKNOWLEDGMENTS

This book could not have been completed without my clients. They were the ones who allowed me to try new approaches to the design of landscapes and gardens and, when finished, photograph them and include them in publications. My heartfelt thanks go to those who were so patient with me when I made errors or when plants would unaccountably die or newly spread soil wash away in a sudden summer storm.

Secondly, I express grateful appreciation and thanks to my friend, Professor Sean Sculley of the Cooper Union in New York City, who wrote the introduction and who gave me much helpful advice.

Thirdly, my thanks go to Randl, Alan and Stephen Bye, my three nephews, who did all the printing of the photographs, to Kendra Lahr for the typing of the manuscript, to Mr. & Mrs. John R. Gaines who loaned me useful reference books from their library, and to many members of my staff who I neglected so I could venture away from my office for picture taking.

Lastly, my thanks go to hundreds of my students who over a period of thirty years constantly encouraged me.

Copyright© 1983 by A.E. Bye

Library of Congress Cataloging in Publication Data

Bye, A. E. (Arthur Edwin)
    Art into landscape, landscape into art.

    1. Landscape architecture--United States.
2. Landscape architecture--United States--Pictorial
works.   3. Bye, A. E. (Arthur Edwin) I. Title.
SB472.32.U6B93 1983   712'.0973   82-22406
ISBN 0-914886-19-3
ISBN 0-914886-20-7 (pbk.)

PDA Publishers Corporation
1725 E. Fountain
Mesa, Arizona 85203

This book is dedicated to my students

INTRODUCTION
by Sean West Sculley, Architect

Gardens form the exquisite link between ourselves and the surface of the earth and, with grace, orient us to the larger design and mystery of the cosmos. Gardening is an art of unification and reconciliation. Without the garden's pleasures and broad understandings, we abandon ourselves and the earth to scurrility. Without gardens, says Bacon, "Buildings and Palaces are but gross Handyworks." How grim the evidence of this fair truth. But then how promising the garden idea; and how necessary the craft and art of gardens.

As one of American's leading landscape architects — or, if I may, "Gardener" for its older and broader provenance — A.E. Bye presents us with examples of his work which constitute an original contribution to his art and profession. Because his work respects the great themes of his art, the principles which shape and support it can be viewed as traditional — that is, with lasting application. For Bye's work bears the qualities of many great gardens: simplicity of concept and design; the discrete use of plants; and a creative dependence on the site. Spare as these principles may seem, they do not negate subtlety and variety of effect nor uniqueness of solution. In fact, it is the steady application of this principle in combination with talent and experience, which account for the happy landscape transformations in Bye's work.

All the projects in this book, incidentally, are of a scale that can be managed and appreciated by the home gardener and not only the professional. They illustrate that once the landscape problem is understood, that is, once the site is divined, and the design set, solutions can be direct, economical and satisfying. Both the means and results of his work are attainable. But we are cautioned by Sir George Sitwell that "The sublime is within reach of a few" while "the beautiful" may be in reach "of many."

When Bye has completed a garden, we have two impressions, each balancing the other: the apparent inevitability of the solution as if some vague expectation had been delightfully fulfilled; and, living in the garden as it matures, a sense of timelessness. We are both reassured and refreshed.

Look, now, at three examples of his work.

A low area, wet and crowded with brush was selectively cleared, and culled — not drained — so that the salient features, such as the Tussock Sedge, which gives the bog its identity, are revealed. Now, depending on the time of the day, we sense in this tufted landscape mysterious and mischievous qualities. Land once called derelict and problematic reassumes its distinct presence. The removal of extraneous rather than the addition of the new governs the execution of the idea.

New England bog

Site of Long Island House

What were minor discrepancies in grade on an otherwise innocuous Long Island House site have been gently shaped and elevated into land swells that, when in shadow, increase apparent depth and distances. The site is expanded. The unending curves reiterate the profile of the native Bayberry and set off the dark tree line which Bye etches contrapuntally with white verticals of Birch. The new ground forms play the snow into long svelte patterns of light against the dark winter earth. Here, the given site is slightly modified rather than drastically rearranged.

On a grander scale, a new stone wall is alternately cut into and lifted above a hill's broad slope, the curve of the wall insinuating the hills' contours and section. It both divides and seams the land, becoming its own shadow and brings the old trees on the hill into a new cadence with each

Curving stone wall

other, making them allies with the distant fabric of the fenced-in fields. Carelessly laid-out, this wall would be a bellicose intruder. Here a single element diplomatically unifies a variety of seemingly unrelated parts.

Observe that each design is decisively governed by a clear concept of what should be done. Details follow. This effort is overseen by Bye's commitment to transmit through the design the latent character of the site — that is, to accentuate or modify, rather than displace what is given.

This attitude of abiding comfortably and patiently with the site is certainly consistent with critical ecological imperatives and the practices of ancient husbandry. It also allows us to make, over time, sympathetic association with his predecessors — say, the eighteenth-century's Repton; the nineteenth-century's Downing and the twentieth-century's Jensen. Thus, we find, with pleasure, loyalties to the broad gestures of sauve Georgian "Land Skips," an interest in the propriety of effects which Downing and Olmsted espoused; and a sensibility which mirrors Jensen's affections for the smallest living details of a particular place. It is this last quality, the affection for the particular, of "close observation" (an artistic habit of the great Dutch landscape artists and many American nineteenth-century painters) — call it watchfulness — which Bye has also practiced with the camera. Bringing together a beautiful recollection of the landscape, he has made a ritual for years of "listening," as Claudel said, "with the eye." This has been Bye's ongoing Grand Tour.

Here are some pictures from that journey.

New England coast *Slave fence in Kentucky*

Bog near Bedford, New York

Amenia Hills, New York　　　　*Montgomery Woods*

We might pair some of these images with the examples of Bye's projects above. But these resemblances show more: Bye's habit of watchfulness and appreciation permits him to assay and respond to a range of landscapes and elucidate their capabilities with apparent intuitive ease. But, intuition is funded by experience, and it is no doubt, the reward of the skillful — that skillfulness borne of "the perception, and so to the enjoyment, of subtler relations which, without study, might go unseen."[1]

Many of the qualities of his work can be attributed to the syncopation of witnessing-discovering, and designing-making. We see now that his design efforts are also conscious and deliberate acts of appreciation. His gardens are a record and response to, and a conscious search for, as he would say, the particular and special mood of the landscape.

The reading of a mood in nature, the sympathetic recognition of self in relation to place, has ancient symbolic and geomantic ancestry with its literary and theoretical antecedents culminating in the nineteenth–century doctrines of association. However, Bye's interest in the diversity of landscape phenomenon results in categories of curiosity and acceptance rather than awe and transcendence.

Wry and pragmatic, this attitude not only has practical consequences, but also leads to a broad and poetic concept of garden and landscape design. Practically, Bye is likely to favor a few tough plants indigenous to the environs and use them for their lasting structure in the design. These he would choose over a more ostensibly fetching assortment of less dependable and possibly exotic varieties.

Conceptually, as we have seen, this method, or devotion to delineating and intensifying the mood of the site, whether a small garden or hundreds of acres, obviates distracting themes and extraneous material, even though Bye joyously celebrates the ideosyncratic. Though his work is decorous, he makes no coy decorations. We are invited by his landscapes to dwell within their domain, rather than carp as onlookers: "It may be argued that real beauty is neither in garden or landscape, but in relation of both to the individual, that what we are seeking is not a scenic setting...but a background for life."[2]

The timeless effect of Bye's landscape work, with its appeal to the mind and senses of the garden dweller, and its refreshing and unpretentious character is summed up in a graceful appreciation by Mary Van Rensselaer of another garden, made by another artist: "He would accept Nature's frame, outlines and materials, and paint his pictures to her local specifications. He would strive to reunite her 'scattered excellences,' but not all of them, and not an assortment chosen at random, only such as she herself might have brought harmoniously together and disengaged from encumbering details, were she able to make pleasure grounds instead of wild landscapes merely. He would respect, preserve, heighten, accentuate, civilize and yet poeticize the natural character of the special site he had chose, and thus would produce not only a good work of art but one with a special local personal charm, inimitable anywhere else."[3]

That which is appropriate is also propitious.

[1]Hubbard, Henry VIncent and Kimball, Theadora. *An Introduction to the Study of Landscape Design.* Boston: Hubbard Educational Trust, Reprint 1959. (1917)

[2]Sitwell, Sir George. *On the Making of Gardens.* New York: Charles Scribner & Sons, Reprint August 1951 (London 1909)

[3]Van Rensselaer, Mrs. Schuyler. *Art Out of Doors.* New York: Charles Scribner & Sons, 1893-1925

PREFACE

Students have asked me how long it takes me to see, in my mind's eye, an idea for a garden. When I reply "about two or three seconds," they are astonished, but I go on to explain that I have visual imagination and can "see" a landscape composition all completed, not down to details, but to the general outlines and forms.

Many factors contribute to my vision of a landscape: training, knowledge, experience, inspiration and principles of design are important, but above all the existing conditions found on a site suggest the final composition.

For example, a site can have gnarled and contorted oaks, twisting against the sky, and suggesting the possibility of stretching the weird scene into a garden of the grotesque. On the other hand, a landscape with violent outcroppings of rock may suggest a landscape of the brutal; or a landscape with a quiet pond may be the point of departure for a garden of serenity.

I have mentioned three kinds of landscapes that suggest mood: The grotesque, the brutal and the serene. In this book I submit to the reader the idea that a landscape can have a mood as a theme. In addition to those moods mentioned above, other examples of mood illustrated in this book include assertiveness, complexity, dazzle, delicacy, fragility, humor, liveliness, animination and gaiety, sensuousness, softness, stability and mystery.

Although I have designed landscapes millions of dollars in scope, I have found the creation of a residential landscape more often a better vehicle to express an idea or concept. I must admit that ideas come from me more intuitively than intellectually when I design a project: The intuitive way is valid, yet the intellectual process also plays its role. The client's needs and desires, the budget, the restraints of law, the restraints or opportunities of ecological conditions and the environment must all be considered. Actually the more factors entering into the design process the easier it is to conjure the vision of the completed landscape.

I have made this preface short. Why? This book is a visual communication, as it should be, and I hope you will agree.

DEFINITION OF LANDSCAPE ARCHITECTURE

The landscape architect must consider the relationships between a building and it surroundings, the topography, orientation, walks, roads, and planting. He must be aware of the influence exerted by climate, and the relationships of earth, plants, water and building materials in space to create an architectural landscape integrated with the natural and man-made environment.

A.E. Bye

CONTENTS

1.1

Figures 1.1-1.3 *Three views to the west showing how the subtle shadows reveal every nuance of the delicate grading.*

The Bayberry appear larger than they really are because there is no human artifact nearby to give correct scale. This results in the illusion of greater space to the serene quality of the lawn.

SOROS

The central idea for the undulating ground forms in the Soros landscape in Southampton, Long Island, grew from the client's desire to have an open rolling landscape similar to the one that he admired in England. Aware of the porosity of the sand-grave-loam soil of his four acre property, he accepted the concept of spatial motion generated by subtle hills, valleys, ridges and depressions seen mostly in profiles of varying lengths against walls of dark foliage on the edge of the clearing.

The landscape was developed by the "hands" of machinery whose movements were directed by our landscape architect, Peter Johnson. For six weeks a bulldozer and a grader shifted the subsoil until the profiles slowly emerged as soft and sequential lines flowing with steady assertiveness past existing grouplings of native Bayberry. The long, streaking shadows of tall nearby trees at the edge of the property rose and fell with the new contours, accentuating the undulating plain.

The landscape's abstract patterns of melting snow in winter are similar as those we see a million-fold on fields and meadows. Here is a startling manifestation, not only of molding land, but of nature, too. We can call this a happy accident, of course, but we, as landscape architects, should not be too surprised, if we are all observant, by the seasonal changes. Each thaw brings new abstractions. And if we design for this, couldn't we call this a timeless aspect of our art? It was also our conscious effort to create a landscape for saving precious rain. Why let it run to the sea when we desperately need to maintain a high water table? With a porous soil below, we conducted run-off to the lowest depressions suitably equipped with basins for underground seepage. This four acre landscape was designed for a family of four living in a man-made town in a man-made landscape. It followed that it be wholly man-made, except for living plants, to create a space of motion and rhythm, of subtlety and serenity. (Peter Johnson, staff landscape architect)

1.2

1.3

1.4

Figures 1-4-1.5 *Looking east we see another aspect of the grading; profiles of contouring and shadows. Fortunately there is a dark background of Evergreen trees at the edge of the property to etch out the highest mound.*

4

1.5

1.6

Figures 1.6-1.7 *At the edge of the property it is the tree shadows that become the dominant elements.*

1.7

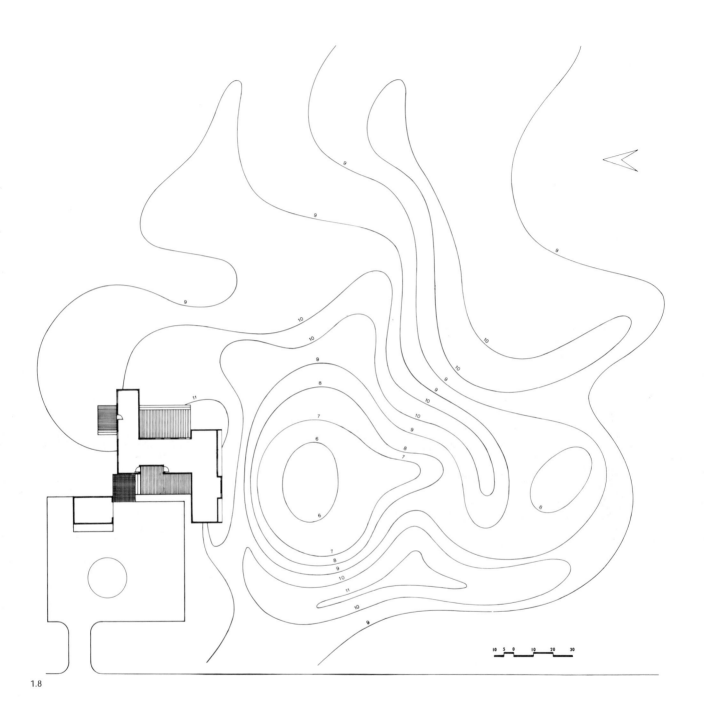

1.8

Fig. 1.8 *The Soros plan*

8

1.9

Fig. 1.9 *Looking towards the same scene as found in Figure 1.6 the landscape composition is changed dramatically by the pattern of melting snow.*

1.10

Figures 1.10-1.11 *The landscape, for a brief time, becomes sinuous as the snow slowly melts. Another but similar pattern will emerge at the next snow melt, creating another landscape composition.*

1.11

1.12

Fig. 1.12 *The inspiration for the Soros landscape came from this view of Amenia Hills, New York.*

REISLEY HOUSE

In the fall of 1951 or the spring of 1952 I was commissioned to solve some crucial landscape problems for a Frank Lloyd Wright designed house in Pleasantville, New York. Since 1951 was the year that I started in independent practice, to be given the opportunity to landscape a just completed Wright house put me to "walking on air." "How could I be so lucky," I said to myself.

It was easy for me to know what to do for a landscape scheme. I had been acquainted with the career of Mr. Wright for years, even during my boyhood. Frank Lloyd Wright's sister, Jane Porter, was my Sunday school teacher and close neighbor in Swarthmore, Pennsylvania, and often, when Wright came to Swarthmore to visit his sister our family would meet him. So, during my college days, when I was studying landscape architecture at Penn State, I steeped myself in Wright's philosophy and architecture, visiting his projects in and around Chicago and the important ones in Pennsylvania.

The commission lasted for several years because the house was enlarged with a bedroom wing for the children of the client, and this caused more landscape work for me.

Briefly, my approach was to use native plants, those that I found growing locally or that I knew to be native to the Appalachian Mountains. Wright had done this at Fallingwater in Bear Run, Pennsylvania. When I visited this inspiring place I was impressed that the landscaping was mostly done with the native Rosebay Rhododendron (Rhododendron maximum) prevailing in that area. Fallingwater was the key that led me to believe that I should follow this example for the Pleasantville house or any house that was built among native vegetation.

2.1

Fig. 2.1 *The view from the edge of the property showing how the house was nestled among the native trees without injuring them.*

2.2

Fig. 2.2 *The view from the terrace where the owners could look upon the "Common" that was left undisturbed by the USONIA community. The predominant plants are Sumac, Bayberry, Gray Dogwood, Gray Birch and Little Bluestem Grass.*

2.3

2.4

2.5 *Wright provided a pocket in the terrace where a specimen Mountain Laurel* (Kalmia latifolia) *could be planted.*

PHILOSOPHICAL STATEMENT

To create effectively, the landscape architect must work outdoors to "feel" each rock and stone, the trees and vines, sand and earth, the sky and water, reflecting light and shadow, the mist, the snow and ice, the rain, the wind and the odors and the noises that are all about us.

HARVEY HUBBELL

When you look at these photographs you may wonder what, if anything we did. If this is so, that is exactly the impression we wanted to make.

These scenes exemplify a philosophy of design that our office has followed for many years: of using native plants for all projects where they can possibly be used.

We go quite far with this philosophy, bringing the native woods or fields up to and against the building walls. This concept comes not from us but from the many clients who want to "go back" to nature. This means the elimination of lawns and all the hard work and cost that goes with them, the elimination of plants that need trimming, cultivating, watering, etc., or anything that needs considerable maintenance. There is, of course, some maintenance: picking up fallen branches, removing excess foliage, or replacing dead or dying plants. Yet, if there is an old hollow tree that is a home for birds and animals, that particular tree is saved.

In the Harvey Hubbell project, we had a client and an architect who thought exactly as we did: they both wanted to bring the native Hemlock-hardwood forest back to the building wall. Here we actually rolled up sections of the forest floor as we would sod, unrolled it on plywood panels, carried it to the site, then slipped it off and planted it. We had 100 percent survival with Canada May Flower, Partridge Berry, Ferns, Club Mosses and seedling Hemlocks, and Birch which the sod contained. (Bruce Campbell Graham, architect; Armistead Browning, staff landscape architect)

3.1

3.2

Figures 3.1-3.5 *The entrance turn-around with accommodations for six cars. It is surrounded on three sides by the native New England woods that seldom needs maintenance care. The flower bed in the center, however, is frequently replanted for color change from spring through fall.*

3.3

Figures 3.4-3.7 *Four views to illustrate that the Client, the Architect and the Landscape Architect worked harmoniously to key the New England woods close to the building edge. This in turn gave the corporate employees a rich and lush scene to enjoy just outside their windows.*

3.4

3.5

3.6

3.7

3.8

Figures 3.8-3.9 *At the executive wing a small geometric terrace was planted densely with Rhododendron and Leucothoe for the purpose of privacy and isolation from the general staff.*

3.9

Figures 3.10-3.11 *The interior courtyard was planted only with native New England vegetation. The ground was covered with Partridge Berry, taken up from the woodland floor nearby, and placed like sod at the base of all Mountain Laurels and Allegany Serviceberrys that constituted the major grouping.*

Later, voids in the Partridge Berry ground cover were filled with Canada May Flower, native ferns, and club mosses to develop a "tapestry" on the ground.

3.10

3.11

3.12

Fig. 3.12 *This typical New England country scene was the source of inspiration for the Hubbell project.*

WESTCHESTER REFORM TEMPLE
Scarsdale, New York

The Westchester Reform Temple was one of my earliest commissions. I worked directly with Marcel Breuer and William Landsberg, the architects for the Temple. Our phliosophy was to use trees of the same kind found on properties surrounding the project. They were Gray Birch *(Betula populifolia)*, Flowering Dogwood *(Cornus florida)*, and Red Maple *(Acer rubrum)*. Fortunately we were able to create an unusual effect by using the white barked Gray Birch against the white sides of the Temple. In winter the effect became more pronounced with the Gray Birch on the white snow: white on white on white. On sunny days the added dimension of shadows became important as they played across the building surface from early morning to about 3:00 in the afternoon. (Marcel Breuer and William Landsberg, architects; Irving Herrmann, partner, landscape architect)

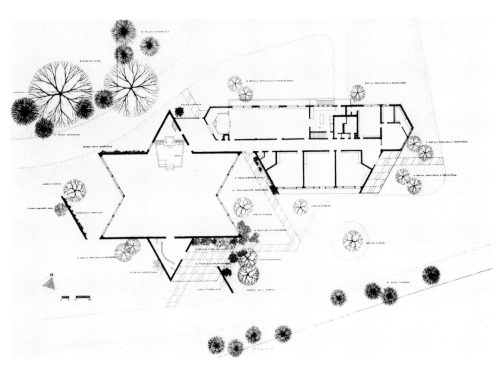

4.1

4.2

Figures 4.2-4.4 *Marcel Breuer, who was refreshingly articulate, believed two were better than three; thus the two Gray Birch and the two Dogwood (Fig. 4.4).*

4.4

4.5

4.6

Figures 4.5-4.6 *Two views. On the entrance side we planted two Cutleaf European Birch (Betula pendula 'Gracilis') under planted with Spreading English Yew (Taxus baccata repandens). Notice the contrasts: horizontals against verticals; dark forms against white; evergreens against deciduous.*

4.7 *Source of inspiration for the Westchester Reform Temple were these Canoe Birch (Betula papyrifera) growing along the Taconic State Parkway, New York.*

SILVER

The inspiration for the Silver residence came to me during a long weekend visit to Monhegan Island off the coast of Maine. Common Juniper grows like a thick carpet along the open rocky coast, together with slim Spruce and jagged Fir, forming an evergreen composition of serene grandeur. The scene, twisted and tortured by the cruel winds from the sea, made a strong impression upon me. I interpreted the visual experience as the inspiration I sought and proceeded, in my mind's eye, to compose the forms for the Silver garden.

The first consideration was the creation of a garden of substantial unity that would grow lush, stay in scale over the years, require little maintenance, and have a quality of space that would be intimate, colorful and welcoming.

Unity was achieved by using various conifers with a similarity of texture: Japanese Red Pine, White Pine, Japanese Black Pine, Limber Pine and Spanish Fir; for ground cover: Shore Juniper (*Juniperus conferta*), Andorra Juniper and Sargent Juniper; for accents: Spreading English Yew.

Having achieved unity of texture and an attendant sense of of serenity, we felt free to lightly add Thyme, Arenaria, Sedum and Festuca for detail and intimate interest along the walks. All these plants are appropriate to the existing dry condition, needing no trimming or pruning to maintain scale.

As work in the garden progressed, we fortuitously exposed outcroppings of rock. This gave us the chance to begin our statements of contrast: the hardness of rock, the softness of plants, the verticality of the pines, the horizontality of the junipers, the greater walk, the lesser walk, the masses and the specimens, and plants against architecture separated cleanly by a gravel moat.

Our statement of space was created by the walls of irregularly shaped pines projecting perpendicularly from the house.

The sense of mystery was created by a curving walk disappearing into pine foliage, and the sense of welcome and warmth by heavy slabs of existing copings placed longitudinally in the front walk.

The sense of stability was established by exposing heavy boulders anchored in the soil, and the sense of place by building a stone fence by the auto turn-a-round.

The sense of permanence was evoked by using slow growing ground cover, and the sense of mellowness by using old weathered stone. (With Irving Herrmann, partner)

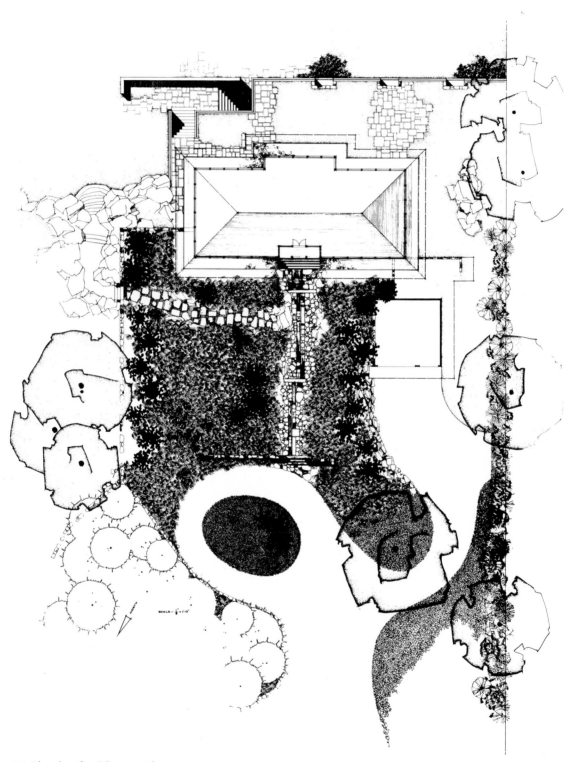

5.1 *Plan for the Silver residence*

5.2

Fig. 5.2 *The huge granite steps were found among wreckage caused by demolition of an old house nearby. They were immediately appropriated for only the cost of moving them to the site.*

5.3

Fig. 5.3 *A composition of contrasts: architecture, landscape; softness, hardness; natural outcroppings of stone, man-laid stone; ounces against tons, horizontality, verticality; light values against dark ones. Shadows and sunlight, yet unified by similarity of texture seen in the Juniper and Pine.*

5.4

Fig. 5.4 *A mason contributed his skills to enrich the design of the walk by varying the placement of the stones.*

Fig. 5.5 *A close look at the needle evergreen planting along the front walk. It was logical to use those plants that favored the hot, dry situation that existed in this rocky place. By using only needle evergreens the author was able to create a strong unified effect. Notice that the black green of the Spreading English Yew was included to relieve a certain "dullness" if only Junipers were used.*

5.5

5.6 *Humor? Perhaps. But why not?*

Humor is one of the most illusive of moods. Not easily defined in landscape composition. We must rely on the response of the beholder for the success of this attempt.

5.7

Fig. 5.7 *To instill greater vigor to the erratic movement of the stepping stones, they were laid to protrude above the soil.*

5.8

Fig. 5.8 *The coast of Maine provided inspiration for the Silver landscape.*

MILLER RESIDENCE
CHAPPAQUA, NEW YORK

This is an early commission that dates back to the spring of 1951 when I was still being influenced by the landscape architecture of Frank Lloyd Wright's Fallingwater residence in Bear Run, Pennsylvania. There I could see native plants embracing the architecture and it looked as though no hand of man played a part. Thus, at the Miller residence I followed Wright's natural approach, finding the woods and boulders already close to the house. (Edward L. Barnes, architect)

6.1

6.2

Figures 6.1-6.2 *The front door scene where an element of formalism was created by a clipped panel of English Ivy. (6.1) Then the landscape quickly reverts to naturalism only a few feet away. (6.2)*

Figures 6.3-6.5 *One of my earliest landscapes where the native landscape was preserved right up to the edge of the house. It is primarily seen from the house as a tree top landscape, and of course, one that "moves" whenever the wind presses the boughs and leaves on a windy day.*

Boulders, covered with lichens play an important visual role. They are the elements of permanence against the variables of plant growth.

6.3

6.4

6.5

6.6

Fig. 6.6 *Scene at Cape Cod, Masachusetts, that served as inspiration for the Miller residence.*

77 WATER STREET
New York City

Our central concept for the plaza at 77 Water Street was to bring nature to downtown Manhattan for the many who need to see some *natural* green. We were fortunate that we had space to plant thirty Honey Locusts rather closely together to form a thick sheltering copse on the north side of the building, twenty more for a double row along Water Street and a few single trees on Old Slip. The city welcomed our idea to abandon the thirty foot spacing rule for street trees and we therefore planted them closely together to create a veil of delicate foliage and a filtering canopy against the summer sun. Luminous foliage is also apparent. It results from viewing the translucent foliage against a bright sun and one will sense that it "glows" with light. Everyone sees this startling effect in the woods in the fall. We therefore consciously made it a major element in our design.

To benefit from this strong characteristic of the Honey Locust, we had a lighting consultant design high lighting to produce luminosity of foliage at night. It causes a soft glow to prevade the trees and the effect is warm, friendly and inviting.

Enticement is a strong aspect of the character of the plaza. It is a retreat from the rain and snow of winter, an escape from the burning summer sun, a place to relax and watch the hustle of the Wall Street crowd, to sit and observe the passing parade of humanity, or just read, eat or sleep. Why not? Too many of our plazas are empty spaces – wonderful to look at but no place to sit and tarry awhile. (Emery Roth, architect; Victor Scallo, staff architect of A.E. Bye's office; plan rendering by Jane MacGuiness)

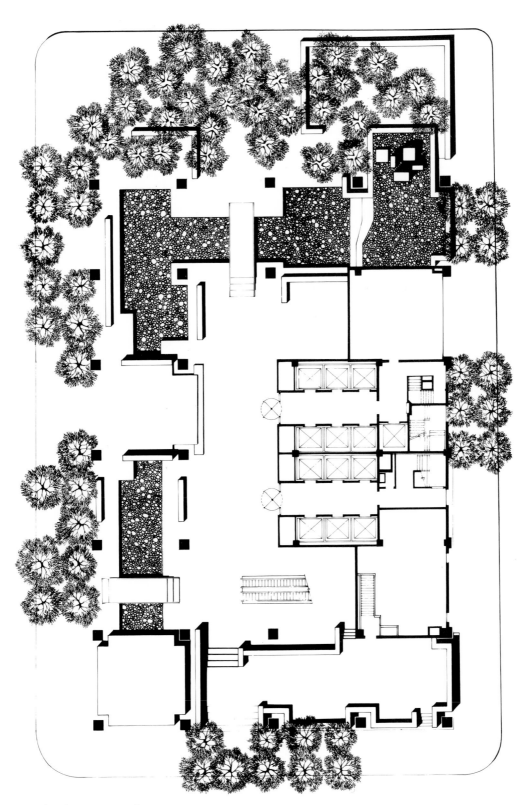

7.1 *Plan for 77 Water Street*

7.2

Figures 7.2-7.3 During lunch time Bennett Park is crowded. Two different kinds of sitting situations were provided: (1) those that want to sit comfortably through a long lunch and (2) for those who want only to rest a few minutes.

7.3

7.4

Fig. 7.4 *This photograph, taken on a sunny Sunday, shows the protective "pocket" where people can relax over refreshments obtained at a kiosk conveniently placed on the property.*

Fig. 7.5 *Another view, on the same day, shows the luminosity of the Honey Locust's delicate foliage. This brilliant effect occurs from about 11:00 A.M. to 2:00 P.M. when the sun beams between the tall buildings that almost enclose Bennett Park.*

Fig. 7.6 *Shadows play a design role, too. On a sunny day they animate the plaza floor, changing as the sun moves.*

Fig. 7.7 *Half the plaza is under the building where infrared ray lamps radiate down from the ceiling, providing some welcome warmth on bitter cold days of winter.*

7.6

7.7

7.8

Fig. 7.8 *Leonardo da Vinci, in his illuminating notebooks, pointed out that certain trees become luminous when they are viewed against a bright sun on a clear day.*

In this portrait of a Sugar Maple we see bright sunlight coming towards us through the leaves to produce this lively and dazzling effect. Scene at Ridgefield, Connecticut

HEAP

The Heap landscape was a result of a complete understanding between the client and the landscape architect of the design philosophy and methods for its accomplishment. The first consideration was that all woods disturbed twenty five feet or more beyond the construction area of the house were to be restored to a close semblance of the previous native condition; the immediate vicinity was to be a direct expression of human effort.

The second consideration was unity. To achieve unity of landscape composition it was necessary to use plants similar in texture to those found in the New England woods of that area and to use boulders, obtained from the site, for supporting the mounds of soil created directly in front of the house. When these elements were completed, there was an indistinct blending of what was man-made and what was natural.

Thirdly, the clients, who would be away for two summer months, needed a relatively maintenance free landscape. Therefore, there was to be no lawn; all bare areas were to be planted with various ground covers: myrtle, ferns, mosses, Maple Leaf Viburnums, and Drooping Leucothoe.

There was one serious problem: obtaining visual security from the entrance to the driveway at the county road. This concern was alleviated by planting two American Beech just above the boulder retaining wall (see photographs). They were dense and large enough to screen the front of the house and to give the visual illusion that the house was pushed back fifty feet from the county road.

In summation, the landscape is an expression of the client's love, respect and understanding of the native environment. He is one who realizes that by working with nature's design a certain serenity, as well as richness of landscape composition, can be achieved. (Ed Paul, architect; David H. Engel, staff landscape architect)

8.1

Fig. 8.1 *Looking towards the house from the country road. Only native New England plants and trees were added to the existing woods.*

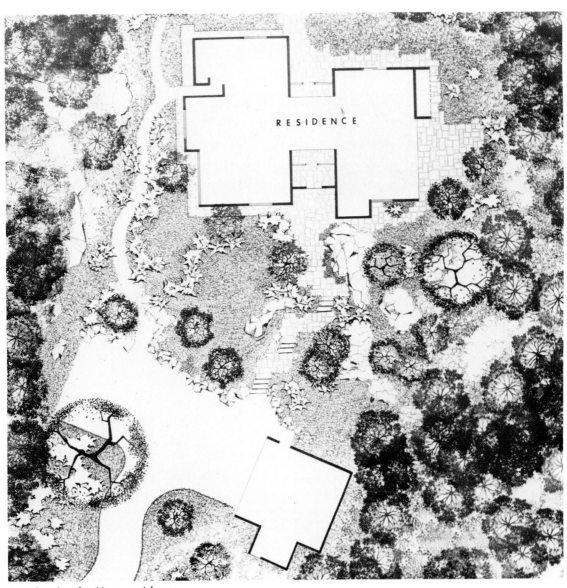

RESIDENCE

8.2 *Plan for the Heap residence.*

Figures 8.3-8.8 *Only those plants that have similar textures to the surrounding woods were used. This gives coherence and unity to the landscape scene. Three kinds of plants constitute the groupings: Mountain Laurel* (Kalmia latifolia) *Drooping Leucothoe* (Leucothoe catesbaei) *and Myrtle* (Vinca minor).

8.3

8.4

8.5

8.6

8.7

8.8

Figures 8.9-8.10 *Fragile plants can be so hardy that they can reappear year after year giving us a scene of summer delicacy. Illustrated are Canada May Flowers (perennials) that become permanent ground covers in woodland areas. These can be found in abundance around the Heap residence. (Scenes found in the Montgomery Pinetum, Greenwich, Connecticut)*

8.9

8.10

MONTGOMERY RESIDENCE

The A.E. Bye and Associates' design for the front entrance and driveway area of the Montgomery residence exhibits an exuberant and imaginative display of rocks and woodland plants to define this vehicular and pedestrian space. The circular driveway surrounding the front entrance is enclosed by a mass of ericaceous plants (Rhododendrons, Mountain Laurel, Drooping Leucothoe) designed to stand out against the dark forest. A slight clearing was established to provide a spatial separation, thus setting a stage for these free-flowing, coarsely outlined plants. Energetic broadleaf evergreens assume command of their position, creating a lush and rolling foundation out of which the multi-branched, Downy Shadblows and tall, straight oaks rise. The tree structure is clearly visible, silhouetted against the dark background and accented by the rough textured foundation leaves.

The use of a pronounced stone edge creates a distinctive separation from the gravel surface and the forest border. This slate rock arrangement varies in height, length, mass, and angle, providing a strong visible impact, but one that also achieves a successful transition from the pedestrian/vehicular space to the background forest. The careful juxtaposition of all these elements combines to form an elegant and distinctive statement in this woodland setting.

In the design for the front entrance of this large estate we had the opportunity to exhibit the individuality of plants within a species. To do this, we chose the summertime, when the background woods would be an even darkness against which to etch the outline of the various plants along the driveway. The reader should observe, in this composition, that the negative spaces are visually equal in importance to the positive forms of the plants. The elements play back and forth before our eyes; we can look at the composition either way.

In winter, of course, we see a different scene, the calligraphy of bare twigs and branches vibrating against the sky. But who should mind; the change makes the landscape that more interesting.

9.1

Figures 9.1-9.3 *Three views showing how the summer woods in the background plays the role of a dark void in support of the feathery positive forms of the trees and Rhododendrons in the middle foreground. THe horizontal rocks become the stabilizing element in this composition.*

9.2

9.3

9.4

Figures 9.4-9.6 *Three views to show the importance of using plants of similar texture to achieve visual unity. In the scenes above Rosebay Rhododendron, Leucothoe, Flowering Dogwood, and Allegany Serviceberry, are loosely grouped around the house and garage.*

9.5

9.6

Fig. 9.7 What makes this woodland scene so eerie? The shimmering thin mist? The vine festooned trees? The multitude of values? The theatrics of the composition?

9.7

Jane MacGuiness

THE STEIN BOG
A New England landscape that maintains itself

In our part of the United States we find many residential clients asking us to design their grounds in such a way that maintenance is almost zero. This is not anything new, but very often they suggest the natural look, whether it be a meadow with high grass and wildflowers, or a woods, or a pond with cattails and water lilies, or a stream bordered with Gray Dogwoods, Spice Bush, Summersweet, Viburnums and ferns, or simply a bog that they often saw from back roads and old lanes. Maintenance firms are disappearing, and if they are to be found at all they often lack skill and knowledge in handling plants. What are we to do? We can get direct inspiration from Nature. Jens Jensen of Wisconsin was a landscape architect who received inspiration from the prairie and indeed, his own home, "The Clearing," in Door County, Wisconsin, was a splendid example of expressing the local ecology.

A woods left undisturbed will sustain its character for years and years. Natural vistas will be viewed with serenity knowing that little, if any, work needs to be done for their continuance. This approach implies looking to the native condition for design ideas, rather than to foreign ones. Why plant exotic trees that will disturb the natural character of a region and possibly be unsuited to the climate and soil? One need only to consider the Maine Coast, as a correct example, or the quiet simplicity of Vermont valleys where rolling fields stop short of steep mountain slopes.

We are finding conservation groups springing up everywhere, concerned with areas in their neighborhood that may possibly be crushed by the bulldozer. All this we know so well, but now we find the home owner, whether he is living in Connecticut or California, looking to nature for landscape effects that can be left alone for years to come.

What are the practical applications of this landscape philosophy? Fewer cultivated flowers to weed, spray, feed and prune, less or no lawn at all to mow, and less worry about hardiness and adaptation of plants to the habitat.

The bog garden illustrated here is a dramatic example of what many of our clients are looking for. Indeed, it was the client who suggested it, finding in the local area such scenes fascinating to contemplate as they change through the seasons. This is an area crowded with wildlife: birds preying upon snakes, the snakes upon frogs, the frogs upon insects, the insects upon micro-organisims, and, the deer roam and various species of turtles crawl.

Our bog landscape was designed by us and it required courageous supervision to execute. Before we could do any construction or clean-up work we had to rid the area of menacing snakes and turtles. Otherwise no laborers would dare enter into the thick mud and ooze. On the first day we encountered seventeen snapping turtles, two Copperheads, and twenty-seven Black snakes. Once the animals were removed without injury to them, we pulled out tangles of fallen branches, old logs and stumps of long dead trees, and began filling in the edges with topsoil for a pedestrian path. Little more was done except for placing some large boulders for stepping stones at visual points of interest and introducing more water tolerant plants like Marsh Marigolds, Cattails, Cinnamon Ferns, Winterberry Holly *(Ilex verticillata)*, Highbush Blueberry *(Vaccinium corymbosum)*, Arrowwood *(Viburnum)*, Red Osier Dogwood *(Cornus sericea)*, and Spicebush *(Lindera benzoin)*. Some Mountain Laurel clumps were planted on higher ground.

Like so many bogs in the New England area, our particular bog has changed very little since 1965, the year of execution. Only an occasional Swamp Maple *(Acer rubrum)* has been removed from year to year to keep the area free from an overhead canopy of darkening vegetation. In the winter the bog has great appeal as the orange color of the Little Blue Stem grass pokes through the snow. This landscape will grow more mellow and stronger as it ages, solving the problems of maintaining a garden while recreating the existing natural look that is now treasured in the mechanized society of today. (Marzell Roming, staff landscape architect)

10.1

Fig. 10.1 *Originally our client wanted a pond. But in my mind this was a little dull, so I suggested saving their existing bog. A short trip to a nearby bog convinced our client to emphasize the one they already had. So all we did was to open it up.*

Figures 10.2-10.4 *The following photographs show the great variety of landscape effects that can be enjoyed by walking around the edge of the bog.*

10.2

10.3

10.4

10.5

Fig. 10.5 *The bog in winter. Tussock Sedge in the foreground.*

Fig. 10.6-10.7 *Bogs in nature which served as sources of inspiration for this project.*

10.6

10.7

RESIDENCE ON THE CONNECTICUT COAST

This commission, executed on a Connecticut shore, is an example of my "handcrafting" the whole project on the site. Except for the winter months, I lived with the clients two days a week for almost two years. Again, we used only native plants found in abundance on the property.

To create the rock formations, I personally tossed every stone and pushed every boulder in as carefree a manner as possible. I tossed the smaller stones over my back letting them fall as illustrated in the inspiration photograph.

This commission allowed me to be a landscape architect as I had envisioned it while still a student: to be outdoors, working with laborers who always seemed so willing to execute my ideas as they came to me, to rise early and work to sunset, to "feel" the plants as I set them out, and a sense of accomplishment at the end of the day.

Figures 11.1-11.2 *For ease of moving outdoor furniture we laid down a large terrace of Bluestone flagstone. The spreading Juniper in the foreground has since made a complete carpet and the meadow in the background has grown higher but not so high as to cut off the view of Long Island Sound.*

11.1

11.2

11.3

Fig. 11.3 *Looking past the master bedroom wing which shows the rocks and boulders freely tumbled into place.*

92

11.4

93

Figures 11.5-11.6 *Two views of the marsh side of the property where only thinning and cleanup were done. The residence is behind the Oak-Shadblow-Wild Cherry woods.*

11.5

11.6

11.7 Source of inspiration: scene on the coast of Maine

COWLES

A.E. Bye and Associates reshaped the contours on the front lawn of the Cowles residence mostly for the fun of it. The client and the designers were weary of seeing new lawns made smooth and even as possible. Why not give a lawn some animation by undulating the surface? The shadows from nearby trees would rise and fall as they extended their way across the heaving lawn. They would change constantly, on sunny days, whether it be winter, summer, spring or autumn.

We were fortunate to have dense existing planting along the property border. The dark plant masses gave sharp definitions to the surface profiles and provided a definite stop to the new contours.

This landscape was not created from following a plan. It was developed on site by our skillful outdoor molder of ground forms, Peter Johnson, who carefully supervised the bulldozer operator for the week or more it took to satisfy the eye from various view points on the property and off. (Peter Johnson, staff landscape architect)

12.1

Figures 12.1-12.2 *Two views of the Cowles garden where the landscape architect departs from the level lawn to create one that becomes sensuous and rhythmic in its heaving forms.*

12.2

12.3

Fig. 12.3 *Scenic area near New Canaan, Connecticut, which served as inspiration for the Cowles landscape.*

GAINES – HA HA FENCE

One spring evening in 1975 my client and I sat on his terrace and gazed northeast to his extensive meadow in the Kentucky Bluegrass country. It sloped downward several hundred feet to a fence in the apex of the valley and then gently upward a thousand feet or more to an open hilltop. As we watched his thoroughbred horses grazing, I asked if the fence was visually disturbing to him. To his affirmative reply, I said, "We can replace it with a Ha Ha fence." Surprisingly, he knew what a Ha Ha was and immediately directed me to build one to eliminate the visual "block" of the wooden fence.

The next day we flew to New York City together, and while on the plane, he asked me how I was going to build it. Having only an envelope in my coat pocket I used it to sketch the serpentine form that would be used, without further drawings, as my guide for staking the Ha Ha in the field.

The fence was profiled to echo the clean rises and falls of the surrounding fields and fences thereon, and the edge of a lake across the valley to the west. Our method of construction was to duplicate the exquisite stone layering of the many miles of stone fences in the vicinity of Lexington, Kentucky. Approximately 450 long, the fence took three months to build and two more months of adjacent grading and sodding to make it "disappear" when viewed from above.

13.1

13.1 *The serpentine form of the Ha Ha fence complements the delicate rhythm of the paddock fences in the far background.*

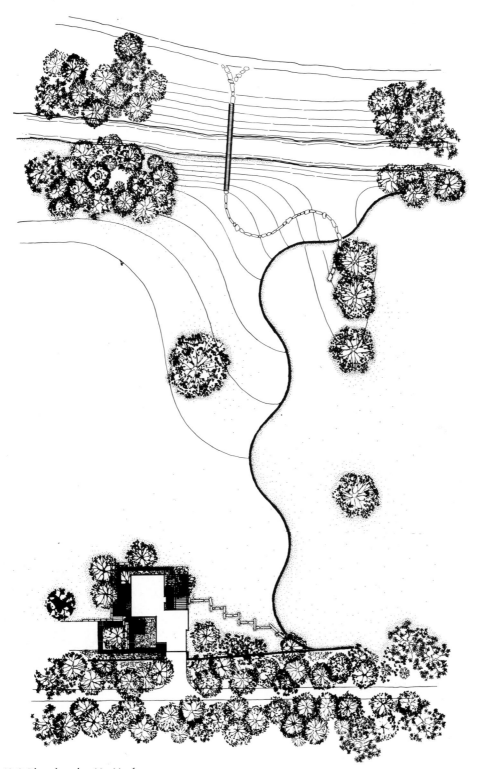

13.2 *Plan for the Ha Ha fence.*

13.3.

Fig. 13.3 *Placement by the author of paddock fences in the fields adjacent to the Ha Ha.*

13.4

Fig. 13.4 *A view towards the meadow showing how the Ha Ha fence merges with an existing old stone fence built many years ago.*

13.5

13.6

Figures 13.5-13.6 *An example where an instinctive approach held sway over an intellectual one—we moved the soil around for weeks to vary the profiles above and below the Ha Ha. The results were tension lines and spaces between the tree shadows, the Ha Ha and the distant top of the hill.*

GAINESWAY FARM–STALLION BARN COMPLEX

I had been working as a landscape architect for the Gainesway Farm in Lexington, Kentucky, for several years when I was asked to design a four stall horse barn to be repeated eight times. I, not being an architect, summoned the aid of Theodore M. Ceraldi, a former Cooper Union student of mine and a former employee. His assignment was to last only five days, Monday through Friday, with a presentation to Mr. and Mrs. Gaines of Gainesway Farm at 8:00 A.M. Saturday morning in New York City. Theodore Ceraldi's design was so exceptional and so correct for the needs of our client that a deal was closed for his services.

From then on it was a collaboration between the client, the administrators of Gainesway Farm, the architect and myself in developing a stallion barn complex for extremely valuable stallions. We were interested in aesthetics; barns suitable for "Kings of the stallion world," as Mr. Gaines put it; and, of course, barns safe and relatively easy to maintain.

The setting for the barns already had a serene quality, the gently rolling open land of the bluegrass country around Lexington. Our approach in siting the barns was to space them rather loosely, avoiding the rigidity of the orthogonal grid, letting them be slightly offset one from the other, keeping the lawns around them relatively free of vertical vegetation to preserve the feeling of the surrounding meadows flowing through.

Our planting concept was based on two premises; first, we wanted safety for the horses, and, second, we wanted trees considered majestic, "kings" of the plant world. We chose Beech of various varieties and the Yellowwood. These were spaced adequately apart from each other to allow for their individual expansive growth in the coming decades.

It must be emphasized here that we were fortunate to have a double row of large old oaks to give a sense of a core to the whole landscape setting. We built a watering trough 172 feet long between the rows of oaks where visitors could assemble, rest on the massive coping, and dip their hands into the cold water on sultry days.

14.1

Fig. 14.2 *The jets were purposely designed to be kept low to avoid exciting the thoroughbreds unnecessarily.*

Fig. 14.3 *Unexpected details become important at night when they are illuminated by floodlights—the lichens on the tree trunks and the texture of the stone coping of the watering trough.*

14.4

14.5

GAINES-FOUNTAIN WALL

At the Gaines residence in Lexington, Kentucky, A.E. Bye and Associates found a spectacular new use for a wall designed to screen the living room from the parking area. The wall became a fountain, spouting and cascading into a stone basin directly below. The Gaines view the fountain primarily in the evening hours, as shown in the night-time photographs.

This fountain wall is constructed of cap stones, salvaged from old areas of Lexington that were undergoing renovation, and from stones found on the Gaines property. The wall is approximately thirty feet in length, eight feet high and eighteen inches wide. The spouts are placed two feet on center and the water is conducted through copper pipes. The water flow is continuous only in the spring, summer and autumn.

15.1

15.2

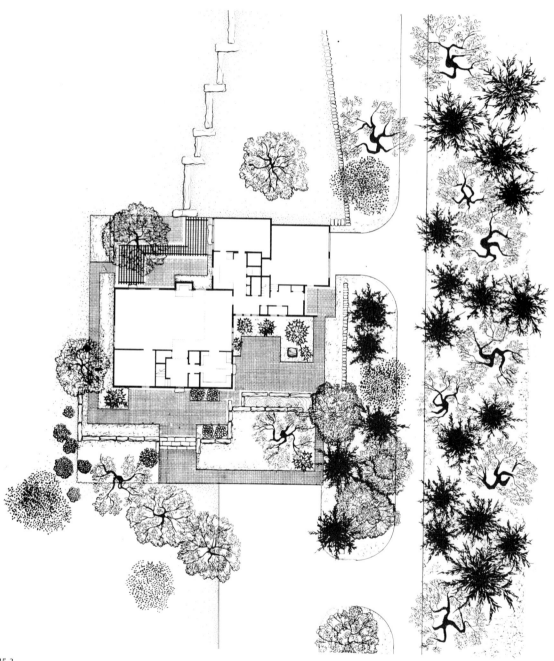

15.3

15.4

SHAPIRO

Many residential clients that come to our office for landscape designs desire a natural approach – a copy, so to speak, of the best of local landscape character. They know from observation that certain native landscapes can continue for a long time with little change, if suitably protected. Thus to simulate such quality of the regional landscape means to them little work, and much enjoyment and a degree of serenity derives from this thought.

When the commission for this residence first came to me through the able and gifted architect Abraham Geller, my first vision was to do a landscape expressive of the heaving, undulating and mysterious sand dunes found along the Atlantic Coast. It would be a landscape serene and tranquil, sequential in mass, but punctuated for contrast by the sharp silhouettes of the Japanese Black Pine, now becoming naturalized in our seacoast landscape.

This was an exceptional site. In the beginning it was all water; the owners planned to fill the eight acres with sand to be sucked up from Barnegat Bay and contained by bulkheading. This was done at a time before public hearings, permits and environmental impact statements.

To do this landscape it was essential to be honest with the natural hardy character of seacoast plants, the softness of sand dunes and the sensuousness of dune grasses. Each much play against the others; the summer black of Bayberry to that of shimmering silver grass; the sharp and assertive pine to the benign edge of dunes, all in contrast to the hard straight lines of house and pool.

The landscape was to billow up and down, with voids and solids, but unified and made coherent by the all prevading grass. "Use only five plants," I said. And so the list was small: Bayberry, Pine, grass, Juniper and "free spun" Yew. Why not more? The ultimate goal was serenity and maybe grandeur. It would be unobtrusive to the sky. Yes, the sky must be this landscape, too. A cogent reason for such a habitat.

The peninsula, the bulkheaded site, was built 400 feet wide and projected 800 feet into the bay. Sand was brought in for several months until we had enough for bulldozers to create mounds and valleys. We never had to worry about drainage, of course, for we knew the rain would pass on through the porous sand.

The house, cabana, driveway, and pool were finished in the early 1950s; two years after the filling was completed, we brought in several thousand Bayberry and a few hundred Japanese Black Pine and disposed them sinuously in undulating masses over and around the domed sand dunes. The dune grasses came from seed already in the sand. Then a wait for a few years for our work to mellow and grow to proper scale. As time went by the pines and Bayberry seeded, further naturalizing our first determinations. Happily the client never diluted or changed our concept with alien plants, understanding sympathetically the serenity and grandeur we achieved. (John Godfrey Stoddart, staff landscape architect)

Figures 16.1-16.3 *Where voids and masses become the dominant elements.*

16.2

16.3

16.4

Fig. 16.4 *The eight foot high Bayberry powerfully channels the entrance driveway. The shadows play a design roll by giving pattern and further horizontality to the horizontal composition.*

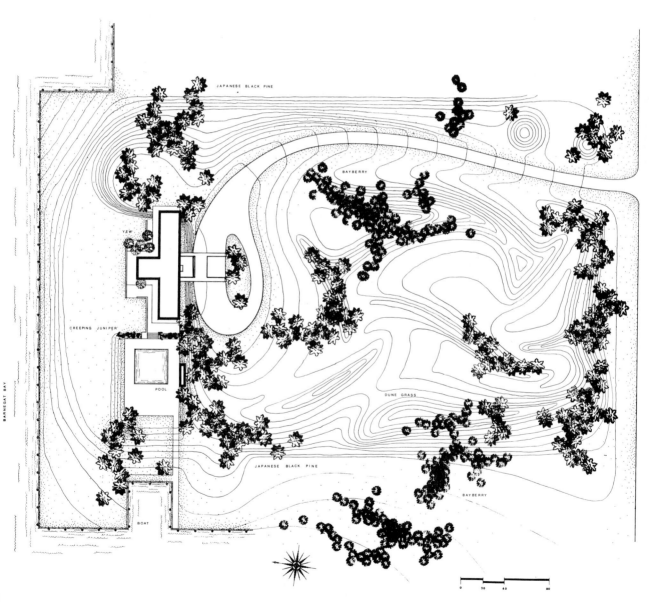

JAPANESE BLACK PINE

BAYBERRY

YEW

CREEPING JUNIPER

POOL

BARNEGAT BAY

DUNE GRASS

JAPANESE BLACK PINE

BAYBERRY

BOAT

0   20   40   80

16.5

16.6

Fig. 16.6 *A detail showing how only two different plants more clearly reveal their character when they contrast in texture, form, and color.*

Figures 16.7-16.8 *Inspriation for the Shapiro landscape came from these sand dunes at Cape Cod, Massachusetts. Not snow, but sand with Bearberry, Bayberry and dune grasses to compose a landscape of stretching softness.*

16.8

JEFFERSON WEST
An office building complex

Jefferson West Plaza was conceived simply as a green space for outdoor relaxation, made lively with a fountain and its cobbled basin, stone sitting walls, a lawn, walk and soft lighting.

A sense of "place" and serenity was achieved by sinking the plaza six feet below the sidewalk level.

Wintertime weather dictated the shallow fountain basin; without the water, the cobbles would be the rough textured carpet constructed for easy sweeping. (Ferry and Henderson, architects; Raymond Smith, staff landscape achitect)

17.2

Figures 17.1-17.3 *A fountain for all seasons. The basin was made only a few inches deep so that in winter, when the water spray was not in operation, pedestrians could stroll across the cobbles. This concept provides for easy maintenance throughout the year.*

17.3

17.4 *Inspiration for this project came from this scene on the Maine coast.*

ARMOUR

The story for this garden is short. The client simply wanted an exuberant garden that was relatively maintenance free. Thus, wherever there was an open space I covered it with an evergreen ground cover, either Japanese Spurge *(Pachysandra terminalis)* or Myrtle *(Vinca minor)* to take the place of a grass lawn. I used the broadleaf evergreens for massing. To keep the broadleaf evergreens from looking too visually heavy, I interspersed deciduous plants: Fothergilla, Winterberry Holly *(Ilex verticillata)* and Flowering Dogwood *(Cornus florida)*. These few last mentioned plants give bright leaf colors during the fall.

It is important, however, that this garden relate well to the surrounding woods. I, therefore, used plants similar in texture to what I found in the woods.

Fig. 18.1 *The predominant plants are the broadleaf evergreens: various varieties of Rhododendron, Mountain Laurel, Japanese Spurge and Myrtle for ground cover, and Leucothoe arranged for a billowy and exuberant display for all seasons.*

18.2

Figures 18.2-18.3 *The court yard is more for looking at than for walking through. These two views, east and west, show native boulders obtained from only a few feet away in the background woods.*

18.3

18.4

Figures 18.4-18.5 *In these two views a small light-colored gravel area can be seen. This is a "void" to counterbalance the all too pervasive dominance of the evergreens.*

18.5

LEITZSCH

The Leitzsch landscape is an example of designing with nature at an intimate scale. The site is located on a craggy promotory in western Connecticut where twisted and jagged Chestnut Oak and heavy masses of Mountain Laurel dominate the rocky terrain. At the edges of naturally open areas of grass and wild flowers stand old White Pine, silhouetting their broken tops against the sky. And all through the woods wild flowers can be found in great profusion.

On this landscape the house was built with consummate care so that the natural beauty was saved within a few feet of the house. The Mountain Laurel, that was given special care, billowed in impenetrable thickets around the Chestnut Oak, and it was our opportunity to cut a maze of paths through them to reveal the ground-hugging plants that gave exquisite detail to the forest floor.

Where there were open glades we left them alone; we needed them to contrast with the confinements of the narrow paths through the Mountain Laurel. And in these spaces we could more easily see the native ferns, mosses, lichens, Canada May Flowers, Trilliums, and the uncovered surfaces of rock outcroppings and boulders. To follow through with preserving the native condition, we left downed trees where they fell, dead branches hang as they died on trees, the fallen leaves piled on the forest floor.

On close analysis, the landscape compositions we created were the result of subtractions, rather than additions. Only near the house were Canadian Hemlocks planted. This was done to develop some visual security from nearby houses that could be seen in winter.

Fig. 19.1 *A view toward the house to show how it relates to the erratic landscape.*

19.2

Fig. 19.2 *Where a small "room" was made by removing a few too closely massed Mountain Laurel.*

142

19.3

Fig. 19.3 *A scene showing how broad-leaved and needle evergreen keep the landscape visually strong in winter.*

19.4

19.5

Figures 19.4-19.5 *For a tight relationship between walk and naturally occurring boulders only stones quarried from the site were used. Most were over 6 inches in depth and solidly embedded in stone dust. Topsoil was sprinkled between the stones to encourage moss to grow. The client built this path from native stone quarried on the site.*

19.7

Fig. 19.6 *The landcape, this time, is the animation of the sheltering tree tops clearly outlined against the sky.*

Fig. 19.7 *A view from the living room showing the drama of the rock ledge rising between the delicate Red Maple, Sweet Birch and Mountain Laurel.*

19.8

Fig. 19.8 *A rugged landscape where the individuality of elements are expressed; the rock outcropping, the Mountain Laurel, the twisting trees, the leaf pattern, and the tree shadows.*

148

19.9

Fig. 19.9 *Although not apparant it is here that the author did selective thinning to reveal the stronger components: Mountain Laurel, rock ledge, fallen leaves and Red Maple.*

19.10

Fig. 19.10 *An opening along a grass path where one can pause to savor the details of the forest understory.*

19.11

Fig. 19.11 *Again, the author isolates native components and reveals otherwise unseen details of the forest floor.*

19.12

19.13

Fig. 19.12 *A Chestnut Oak becomes the turning point along a grass path entering the dark forest.*

Fig. 19.13 *Gaiety in Summer manifested by the bright spots of white flowers of the Maple Leaf Viburnum.*

153

19.14

Fig. 19.14 *The woods in winter offers with considerable clarity the structures of plants. In this illustration every little twig and branch, every shadow, every leaf becomes a vital visual element in contrast to the dark forms of the dominant oaks. A waving motion can be discerned in the arching limbs and the soft horizontal shadows in the foreground. All is etched out in the soft snow and the bland sky. This scene in Ridgefield, Connecticut was the source of inspiration for the Leitzsch landscape.*

HERING PROPERTY
Ridgefield, Connecticut

So often the unexpected occurs in garden construction. While moving soil on the Hering property we suddenly exposed limestone rock formations of astonishing complexity and drama. We therefore had an "honest" rock garden that we treated only with erratic groupings of several kinds of Spreading Juniper. We felt that when the Junipers were in place it was enough for visual interest, and we stopped there.

20.1

Fig. 20.1 *To plant more than what is illustrated here would cover too much of the varied convolutions of the exposed limestone outcroppings.*

20.2

Fig. 20.2 *From this visual vantage point the landscape composition has a strong quality of unity with the rocks all sloping in the same direction.*

20.3

Fig. 20.3 *A study of stability, this time. One should get the impression that nothing could disturb the boulders.*

20.4

Fig. 20.4 *A study of contrasts: ounces against tons; white against dark gray-green, animate opposing inanimate, the temporary opposing the permanent.*

PHOTOGRAPHIC ESSAY ON MOODS

I live on a hill in western Connecticut. In front of my home descends a large meadow to the north and behind rises a thick forest of mixed deciduous trees and native conifers. I spend a good deal of my time at home, especially in the winter when so often the weather is foul.

It was on Sunday afternoon in December many years ago that I was kept indoors by a cold steady rain. Looking through the windows I could see the forest trees all candied with ice from a previous storm. They dripped those million cold drops of water upon the gray crusted snow and their soft sounds made me feel dejected and lonely. To be confined by such a dismal scene turned my attention to the fire in the hearth, where I could sit before it with a good book and a stout whisky.

It is best, though, at a time like this, to turn to contemplation. This day nature presented a gloomy mood. The soggy clouds never showed a brightening break; there was no lessening of the rain. It splattered and streaked the windows, and occasionally the icy branches cracked with a blow of the wind.

"This is a mood of nature," I said to myself. "It is a positive scene; everything is right. Nature is harmonious whether on a dull day or bright." I realized that nature has many moods. In October, when the days are brighter and the sloping rays of the sun fall upon the colored landscape, nature presents a joyous scene. The air is usually dryer, too, and encourages one to a cheerful disposition and a happier state of mind.

It is now a good twenty years since I resolved on that dismal afternoon to search for moods of landscapes. A student of mine studying architecture at the Cooper Union in New York City later fortified this resolve by showing me how the moods could be captured and recorded with a camera as I came upon them in the United States, and the various countries of Europe, South America, and the Caribbean.

I became obsessed with the idea of mood in landscape. I felt it was a great necessity to return to my students each fall with photographs of serene landscapes or humorous landscapes or mysterious landscapes. I came to see that a definite mood could be a landscape theme. Everywhere upon the face of the land or sea or in the sky we can find mood. Upon the surface of the land we find plants, large and small, that evoke or suggest a mood. It may not be readily apparent, but upon scrutiny a mood of some kind will come through, colored by our experiences and past associations. Obviously mood is subjective, and what one person may see as just a gloomy landscape another may see as horrible or terrible depending upon his present state of mind.

It has given me keen pleasure to show these photographs to different people to observe their reactions. Invariably they see more or less than I did and make comments with adjectives that I had not thought of.

I thought of many scenes from my extensive travels; the friendly open rolling hills of central Pennsylvania, the gloomy tangle of the Okefenokee Swamp, the stillness of the Florida Everglades, the grandeur of the Alps, the harshness of the Maine coast, the serenity of Belgium parks, the complexities of the New England woods with their rocks, cliffs and many miles of stone fences, or the stretched-out life of huge Live Oaks in Georgia.

The idea of mood is timeless and universal. We think of parks. The very word conjures in our minds a place to escape from a harrassed life, an environment for relaxation, respite from stress, a change of scene. And the scene does not have to be a tranquil one. It can be one that is grotesque or harsh or sublime, or one of grandeur. We will enjoy the change.

Although, we could describe the moods of nature with many words we can more readily discern moods through our sense of sight. Thus, this book is a pictorial essay. I hope that the many scenes presented here will stimulate the readers of this book, especially those who design with the land, to make closer observations of the moods of nature and discover mood as a unifying element for a landscape composition.

21.1

MYSTERY: American White Cedar Swamp, Woods Hole, Massachusetts
    Brilliant sunshine quickly sinks into the forbidding darkness of the
swamp's black water.

21.2

MYSTERY: Boulder in Woods Hole, Massachusetts
 Why a solitary stone? Why the branches radiating from its
presence? As if it were some source of ominous contamination.

21.3

MYSTERY: Swamp in Ridgefield, Connecticut
  Swamps can be mysterious when much is obscured by heavy vegetation and darkness. Even in winter when sunlight slopes through the naked trees we still find much that is hidden. In this swamp we discern only vaguely what is there. This provokes mystery.

21.4

DAZZLE: A meadow along North Salem Road in Ridgefield, Connecticut

The brilliant luminosity of the autumn meadow stands clearly in contrast to the rugged stone fence and the undulating wall of trees. With a breeze it shimmers to enliven the country landscape even more.

21.5

CLEANNESS: Ridgefield, Connecticut
 In October, when the ground and streams are still relatively warm, I can expect the early morning mist, on certain clear cool days, to drift awesomely through this valley, outlining the soft undulations of the foreground trees.

21.6

CLEANNESS: Sea Coast of Maine
     Here the patterns and textures change, not only by the day, hour and minute, but by the seconds as the waves roll up and slide down at high tide and low tide, stormy weather and mild.

167

21.7

COMPLEXITY—INTRICACY: Black Locust on Cape Cod, Massachusetts
   A striking example of the importance of silhouettes of plants against an evening sky. Portrayed here as erratic movement in the tortured limbs of Black Locust and Honeysuckle vines.

21.8

DELICACY—FRAGILITY: New Jersey Marsh

A watery scene that arouses our acoustical sense. We can "hear" the water lapping, the delicate rushes swishing in the unseen wind, and the occasional sounds of water fowl. Pervading the landscape, however, are the soft sequential forms of the receding islands, evoking serenity and tranquility.

21.9

ELEGANCE: Morris Arboretum in Philadelphia
 Nature as theater where mature trees present their strong individuality as equals. Elegance is expressed two ways; in the graceful fanning of the old Oaks and in the solid verticality of the Spruce.

21.10

ELEGANCE: Montgomery Pinetum, Cos Cob, Connecticut
   A powerful composition of contrasts; the delicate against the sturdy, horizontals against the verticals, light against the dark, the permanent versus the impermanent, the pliant versus the solidity of the old Oaks. Above all, elegance.

21.11

BRITTLENESS: Bonaire, Netherland Antilles
  Too often we say, "It's dead, away with it. Yet in death its "dry bones" of silver gray crack, snap and scrape with the passing wind.

172

21.12

BRITTLENESS: American Beech leaves on the ground
    Have you ever shuffled through the dry, crisp fallen leaves of autumn? Have you looked at their patterns? Their colors? Sniffed their odors? Some remain upon the ground for years. Others vanish with the wind.

173

REFERENCES

Architectural Forum. "Streamlined Factory: White Streak Along the Open Road." Estee Lauder Laboratories, Melville, NY. Davis, Brody and Associates and Richard Dattner, architects; A.E. Bye, landscape architect, March 1967, pp. 76-83.

Architectural Graphic Standards (Seventh Edition). A.E. Bye and Associates contributed 9 pages to Chapter 2, "Site Work – Landscaping." p. 159-170.

Architectural Record. Residence of Mr. and Mrs. Donald Miller, Chappaqua, NY. Edward Larrabee Barnes, architect; A.E. Bye, landscape architect, May 1959.

Architectural Record. "Record Houses of 1969." Mr. and Mrs. Leonard Garment City House, Brooklyn, NY. Joseph and Mary Merz, architects; Paul Gugliotta, structual engineer; McGuinness and Duncan, mechanical engineers; Ben Baldwin and Mary Merz, interior design; A.E. Bye, landscape architect, 1969.

Dictionary of Architecture and Construction. Edited by Cyril M. Harris, Professor of Architecture and Electrical Engineering, Chairman, Division of Architectural Technology, Columbia University and A.E. Bye, FASLA. A.E. Bye and Associates contributed Landscape Architectural Definitions. New York: McGraw-Hill Book Company, 1975.

Garden Design, The Fine Art of Residential Landscape Architecture, Premier Issue. "The Garden in Black and White." Lexington, Kentucky. Design and photography by A.E. Bye and Associates, landscape architects, pp. G-88 to GD-89. Louisville, Kentucky: Publication Board of the American Society of Landscape Architects, 1982.

House Beautiful. Residence of Mr. and Mrs. Morris Winograd, Englewood, NJ. A.E. Bye, landscape architect, April 1958.

House Beautiful. "A House For All Seasons." Residence of Mr. and Mrs. Julius Silver. Roy Sigvard Johnson, architect; Melanie Kahane, decorator; Bye and Herrmann, landscape architects, April 1965.

House Beautiful. "Perfecting an Old Mill – Its New Addition and Romantic Surroundings." Garden of David Whitcomb. David Morton and Thomas Cordell, architects, A.E. Bye and Associates, landscape architects, pp. 76-82, 140, September 1982.

International Who's Who of Intellectuals (Volume 4). A.E. Bye's professional biography, p. 157. Cambridge, England: International Biographical Centre, 1982.

Landscaping. Dorr-Oliver, Inc., Stamford, CT. Bye and Herrmann, landscape architects, September 1960.

Landscape Architecture. "Designing With Plants – Monhegan Island Inspiration." Residence of Mr. and Mrs. Julius Silver, Greenwich, CT. Roy Sigvard Johnson, architect; Melanie Kahane, decorator; Bye and Herrmann, landscape architects, April 1964.

Landscape Architecture. "What You See: Landscape Luminosity," April 1966.

Landscape Architecture. "Shifting Subsoil by Grader and Bulldozer Recreates the Contours of Salisbury Plain." Residence of George Soros, Southampton, NY. A.E. Bye and Associates, landscape architects, July 1969.

Landscape Architecture. "Two by Bye." Harvey Hubbell Corporation, Orange, CT.; Bruce Campbell Graham, architect; A.E. Bye, landscape architect. Heap Residence, Greenwich, CT. Ed Paul, Architect, A.E. Bye, landscape architect, July 1974.

Landscape Architecture. "The Carefree Vista." Shapiro Residence, Long Beach Island, NJ. A.E. Bye, landscape architect, October 1975.

Landscape Architecture. "The Bog – A Landscape that Maintains Itself." Residence of Mr. and Mrs. Howard Stein, North Salem, NY. A.E. Bye, landscape architect, March 1980, pp. 186-189.

Landscape Architecture. "Ha Ha for a Horse Farm." Residence of Mr. and Mrs. John R. Gaines, Gainesway Farm, Lexington, KY. A.E. Bye and Associates, landscape architects, May 1981.

Landscape Design and Construction. "Two East Coast Homes: Opposing Problems." A.W. Geller, architect; A.E. Bye landscape architect, April 1965, pp. 14-17.

Nature's Design – A Practical Guide to Natural Landscaping. Carol A. Smyser and the Editors of Rodale Press Books. A.E. Bye projects illustrated on dust jacket, book cover and pp. XXI and XXIV. Emmaus, PA: Rodale Press Inc., 1982.

New York Magazine. "The Best Street Life in the World: Why Scmoozing, Smooching, Noshing, Ogling are Getting Better all the Time." (77 Water Street mentioned as winner in article by William H. Whyte), July 1974.

Plan Graphics (Compiled by Theodore D. Walker). A.E. Bye projects illustrated on pages 56, 66-76, 110, 111, 113, 127. Mesa, AZ: PDA Publishers Corp., 1977 (2nd Edition).

Plants in the Landscape. By Philip L. Carpenter, Theodore D. Walker, and Frederick O. Lanphear. A.E. Bye projects illustrated on pages 58, 141, 145-148, 152, 178, 186, 190, 313, 343 and 409. San Francisco, CA: W.H. Freeman and Co., 1975.

Progressive Architecture. Annual Awards, Planning and Urban Design, Second Jury. Jerzy Glowczewski, Robert Schofield and A.E. Bye. January 1971.

Progressive Architecture. "77 Water Street – 'There's a Sopwith Camel on the Roof." A.E. Bye and Associates, March 1971.

Progressive Architecture. "By the People." East Orange School Design Center, East Orange, NY. Architects: Uniplan; Jules Gregory FAIA, partner-in-charge; Landon Proffitt AIA, project manager; Robert Hanle, PE, partner-in-charge of engineering; Charles M. Decker and John Ruble, designers; Larry Golblatt, director of EOSDC; A.E. Bye and Associates, landscape architects, February 1972.

Progressive Architecture. "Forest Murmurs." June 1974, pp. 64-71.

Progressive Architecture. "Second Wall House, The Bye House." John Hejduk, architect; A.E. Bye, landscape architect, June 1974.

Progressive Architecture. "A Second Look." Hart Middle School, East Orange, NJ. Architects: Uniplan, Princeton, NJ; Jules Gregory, partner-in-charge; Lawrence Goldblatt, director, East Orange Design Center; John Rubie, project designer; Clifford Marchion, partner-in-charge of construction; A.E. Bye, landscape architect, 1976.

Progressive Architecture. "Fit for a King." Gainesway Farms, Lexington, KY. Theodore M. Ceraldi, architect; Boswell Engineering and Laminated Timbers, Inc., structural for Exercising Ring Building; A.E. Bye and Associates, landscape architects, December 1981.

Residential Landscaping I. By Theodore D. Walker. A.E. Bye projects illustrated on pages 2-5, 15, 45, 194 and 125. Mesa, AZ: PDA Publishers Corp., 1982.

Site Design and Construction Detailing. By Theodore D. Walker. A.E. Bye projects illustrated on pages 54, 87, 129, 130, and 166. Mesa, AZ: PDA Publishers Corp., 1978.

Stone. "Japanese Garden: Imperial House," New York, NY. David H. Engel, consulting landscape architect; Bye and Herrmann, landscape architects, March 1962.

Shopper's Guide, The 1974 Yearbook of Agriculture, United States Department of Agriculture. "The Why and How of Garden Design." A.E. Bye and Armistead W. Browning, 1974.

The New York Times Sunday Magazine. "The New Thrust of Landscaping." Article on the work of A.E. Bye, pp. 66-67.

Time-Life Books. "Easy Gardens." Donald Wyman and Curtis Prendergast. (Two page photograph of the Shapiro Landscape, Long Beach Island, NJ), Alexandria, VA: Time, Inc., 1978.

Time-Life Books. "Landscape Gardening". James Underwood Crockett and the Editors of *Time-Life Books.* (Two page photograph of the Silver Residence, Greenwich, CT., pp. 78-79), Alexandria, VA: Time, Inc., 1971.

Town and Country. "T and C's Guide to the Art of Landscaping." Suzanne Wilding and Anthony Del Balso. Comments on the career of A.E. Bye, FASLA, pp. 82-83, June 1980.

Town and Country. "The Apple's Eden." Article on Central Park in New York City by Wendy Insinger. A.E. Bye quoted on page 192, September 1982.

Who's Who in the East (18th Edition). A.E. Bye's professional biography, p. 114. Chicago: Marquis Who's Who, Inc., 1981.

DATE DUE

SEP 22 '87			
NOV 16 '90			
GAYLORD			PRINTED IN U.S.A.